CREATING YOUR LANE

Unleashing Self-Confidence

Freddi T. Lane

Chasen Dreams Media

*This book is dedicated to those who are
ready to own their greatness.*

CONTENTS

Title Page

Copyright

Dedication

Introduction

Part I: New Beginnings   1

Prepare Your Lane   3

We're in This Together   5

My Journey   8

You Are the Way to Success   12

Part II: Unleashing Self-Confidence   15

Believing in You   16

Emotional Triggers   22

Anxiety   28

What They Say Doesn't Matter   34

Be Bold   41

Eat Some Humble Pie   47

Acknowledgments   52

About the Author   54

Notes   55

INTRODUCTION

I want to take this time to say thank you. I appreciate your willingness to step outside the box and explore the "what if." I am not an ordained religious minister. However, I do believe that I am a minister of empowerment. I believe that each of us holds power in our actions to educate, influence, and lift others. This is the first book of the "Creating Your Lane" series.

It was written to discourage that annoying voice of fear and to provide a direct approach for creating a path towards success. My objective is to engage you to answer the questions in this book while creating a visual plan of what success looks like for you. Answer the questions honestly. There are so many times in life when you should follow your instinct and have faith in your decisions. Use this book and let your intuition takes over. Answer the questions, take notes, identify roadblocks and create your lane to success.

Have you ever wanted to open your own business but did not based on someone else's opinion? Did you stop pursuing your big dreams because of what others said? STOP!! Stop listening to others' views without thoroughly educating yourself on facts. You are intelligent so use your own intellect to determine what is best for you. There are so many resources available to research what it takes to achieve your goals. In addition, stop fighting with yourself and trust your abilities and instincts. Now is the time to go for it!

God has and will continue to provide. He has equipped us with the word and resources to fulfill our dreams. Now let's focus on unleashing self-confidence. In this book, we will go through six steps that help build confidence, including believing in yourself, having faith in yourself, and having positive mindset.

PART I: NEW BEGINNINGS

PREPARE YOUR LANE

Making decisions are part of life. We make impactful decisions several times a day. How do you make decisions? Are they based on what you were taught? Many of us were raised by people who repeated what they learned. As children, we were raised to believe and mimic what our elders taught. Many of us lived the majority of our lives in the lanes of our elders, making decisions based on what our elders did. God created each of us as unique individuals with different gifts. It's time to create your lane. Evaluate your life to determine if what you were taught works in your life today.

Romans 12:6
[6] We have different gifts, according to the grace given us. If a man's gift is prophesying, let him use it in proportion to his faith

WE'RE IN THIS TOGETHER

Above all, we are alive each day by the grace of God. The anxieties and hurdles that we face each day are not new to the world. Daily we awake to a new day. This allows us opportunities to create new beginning or re-write our story.

We all need some form of responsibility to make us accountable so that we are able to move forward and succeed. Responsibility can come in many forms. Setting deadlines for goals so that we can accomplish our dreams is a form of being accountable. Surrounding ourselves with accountability partners, who encourage us along the way makes us responsible. Negative people lingering over you constantly reminding you of past mistakes should not be included as accountability partners.

We all have the ability to beat ourselves and pick out the mistakes we've made in the past while navigating through life. Constant reminders of our shortfalls rarely have a positive impact. This is why we need positive encouragement. However, we must be open to accepting encouragement. We have so little confidence in ourselves that we have discounted ourselves and true worth. We've found it hard to live in our greatness.

The choices that we make can be life-altering. It is easy to shortchange ourselves if we fail to challenge our choices. What should we know if we fall short of reaching goals? What changes can be made so we can continue to win? How do we without hesitation affirm the excellent characteristics of ourselves and others? I've learned that those three questions can be answered in every situation, whether we win or lose. However, we should answer those questions honestly to be accountable for our actions so that we can successfully fulfill our dreams.

God uses us to reveal his word to others. He equips us to help others as well. We carry a measure of uncertainty with every ounce of confidence. Hence, identifying uncertainty is our job. That allows us to build and display confidence outwardly. God gives us grace and healing. Therefore, we should willingly share what we've learned from God with others.

1 Thessalonians 5:11
[11]Therefore, encourage one another and build each other up, just as you are doing.

MY JOURNEY

How did I get here, you may ask? The gift to help people has lived in me for a while. I believe that this gift was passed down to me through a long line of generational genes. Although my approach is different from those before me, we've all sought to help others.

My parents and grandparents served the community faithfully. They empowered others by educating, nurturing, providing shelter, and advocating for families. Their strength and determination made it second nature for me to encourage others to embrace unfamiliar ground and shoot for the stars.

I've found that inspirational approaches that work today to empower people will work in the future. I've learned through having faith, working with others, and living life that having faith in a high power strengths confidence. As I continue researching and documenting experiences, I'm still learning while mastering processes.

There's nothing that we can't do. Often, we are told what we can't do. It puts us in a place of fear. Fear makes us believe that we can't achieve our wants and goals. Some believe that we can't have success without the approval of another person. Success is what you make it. Being told what I couldn't do made me hungry to succeed. Like you, I can do whatever I put my mind to. There are no limits when you have faith.

There's no fast track nor direct approach to making someone

self-confident. Some people are born with confidence and for others, it can take time to develop. Nonetheless having self-confidence comes with knowing and having faith within. Knowing something comes from studying, analyzing, and understanding the paths taken by yourself and others.

I did not complete college. Although I graduated high school, attended trade schools, and held numerous certifications over the years, to some I am considered uneducated. I've been part of conversations where I've been told to shut-up. I've been looked at with the side eye when speaking and told by others that I didn't know anything. When having full knowledge of a particular subject, I've been cut-off while speaking and told by others that I did not know what I was talking about. I've been told personally and professionally that I would not succeed in achieving my goals due to not having a degree. These are the people that I now avoid. Those are the people that did not want to see me win.

I took those negative words to heart and allowed them to kill my spirit. It bothered me that those people thought so little of me. I lived with those words in my heart and head for years. I spent a great amount of time with low self-esteem and little faith. Hearing negative words made me feel less than a person. Not being good enough stuck in my head. This was painful because these things came from women that looked like me. They told me I did not have what it took to lead. Sadly, I was stuck in that place of believing what they thought of me for a while. It took me a while, but in time I reconnected to my "kick butt, I can do it all" spirit. I wasn't going to accept that I was a failure because I knew that was not true.

In my personal life and in my career, there have been people that took the time to offer me positive guidance. They showed me how to get to the next level and introduced me to resources to improve in specific areas of my career and life. I began attaching myself to a diverse group of people. I learned to be truthful with myself and trustful in others. I learned that great teachers do not all look like me.   I listen to the words of positive people. This led me to finding great success and opportunity for happiness and promotion. I've found enjoyment in being around with people who respected and like me. Life became easier when I was around those that treated me with kindness.

Hebrews 10:24-25
[24]*And let us consider how we may spur one another on toward love and good deeds,* [25]*not giving up meeting together, as some are in the habit of doing, but encouraging one another —and all the more as you see the Day approaching.*

YOU ARE THE WAY TO SUCCESS

You are here because you want to know more. You are curious to read about how you can achieve success. Achieving success will be based on what you already know and have within you. The law of attraction is that we can attract the good things our minds create. Like you, I am curious to learn more. We are both here to promote positivity through our thoughts.

We tend to act out what we think is true. These assumptions are based on what we are taught. Disappointment comes from our perception that we've failed. You are not a failure. Once you have confidence in yourself, you embrace change. You can succeed even in the face of failure.

Proverbs 18:15
[15] The heart of the discerning acquires knowledge,
for the ears of the wise seek it out.

PART II: UNLEASHING SELF-CONFIDENCE

BELIEVING IN YOU

What is your passion? Understanding the root of your love may help you unlock your gift. Never dim your light. Your gift or superpower is what you define it to be. Do you know that your superficial characteristics have no worth? It's what's in your heart that matters. God can see your true intentions and will guide you to help others. Speak positivity into your life even when you feel pessimistic. Believe in yourself. That's the number one rule. It doesn't matter what anyone else thinks or whether they believe in you. Whatever is in you fuels your purpose. Never second guess yourself based on others' perceptions. It doesn't matter what your goal is. You can achieve it. Whether it's starting a business, creating a cookbook, raising your children, having a successful marriage, managing your weight, going back to school, or traveling the world. Whatever it is that you want to do, wholeheartedly believe that you can do it. Don't let anyone discourage you.

Success begins when you have envisioned your dream. During the envision phase, you will be able to identify what you want. Create a vision board incorporating the resources and requirements for fulfilling your want and needs. When building your vision board, you will become accountable for taking action toward completing your goals. When you can visualize your dreams, they become more attainable.

Consider a vision board format that allows maximum daily exposure. I recommend digital formats because they can be stored on mobile devices. Copy and paste images to a large workspace when creating your digital vision board. Consider using software and applications developed for building collages and image-editing. After completing your vision board, save it as a screensaver and photo image on your device. Additionally, set a reminder on your device to review the board daily.

Are your dreams and goals clearly defined? Is there a specific dream from your past that you wanted to accomplish but did not fulfill? Dream killers are real. It can be a person, situation, or circumstance. How many times have you been discouraged? How often have you allowed negativity to influence your thoughts? You will need to change your mindset. Surround yourself with positive people that encourage you to be your best. Taking action to fulfill a lifelong dream will never be easy. Most dreams won't have kicker success. There is a chance that you could hit a roadblock when trying to fulfill your dream. However, don't focus on what may not happen. Focus on all the greatness that will occur. It's all in your belief and planning. You have what it takes to make it happen, and having the proper support goes a long way. You are in control of your actions. Your dream will become a success. How can we fail? With God on your side, he doesn't set us up to fail. God gives us everything that we need.

Questions for the Reader

1. *Have you ever tried pursuing a new opportunity but thought you couldn't achieve it? If so, what discouraged you?*

2. *Have you acted on instinct without input from others? How did it make you feel?*

3. *What are three words that scare you? What do these words mean to you?*

4. *How do you deal with unhearing hurtful words?*

5. *Do you feel that you are worthy?*

Joshua 1:9

⁹Have I not commanded you? Be strong and courageous. Do not be afraid; do not be discouraged, for the Lord your God will be with you wherever you go."

Affirmations

I have a clear vision.

I will make the most of new opportunities.

I am following God's path for success and victory.

I am worthy and precious, and my thoughts matter.

I am knowledgeable and successful in all that I do.

EMOTIONAL TRIGGERS

Do you know that your emotions control half of your dreams? What we go through and how we respond in life are based on emotional triggers. It could be how someone approaches or looks at you. Emotions affect you in many ways, causing you to feel joy, sorrow, fear, hate, and even love. How do you deal with negative emotional triggers? Do you know what your emotional triggers look like? Figure out your triggers so that you can move to the next level.

Fearful emotions can delay success and slowly destroy you. This can stop you from achieving so much. How will I feel if I'm not successful? What's going to happen if I fail? How will I regroup after failure? Positive emotions will help settle your fears. That's your reassurance that you can succeed. Have you discovered how to turn those negatives into positives? It's possible. One negative trigger does not have the power to ruin all the positive. Learn to control your emotions and be mindful of what that feels like.

Stop emotional triggers by creating a written plan of action to be used when triggered by negative words or situations. Creating a plan of action to help you get back on track is necessary when creating your lane to success. When building my action plan to stop emotional triggers, I included self-care actions that helped me feel at peace. When triggered by hurtful words, I don't respond to the agitator; I will say the names of people who bring me peace and leave the situation. When irritated by someone's words during conference calls, I doodle, drawing pictures of my favorite time of the year, or will lotion my hands with my favorite scented lotion. I know this may sound crazy. These are my distractions from the negativity. Even if, for a moment, my actions allow me to shift my focus and not respond to the negativity. Don't let those negative emotions interfere or become a roadblock to your success.

Questions for the Reader

1. *Are you still holding onto grudges from your past? If yes, has holding onto the negative made you a better person? Create a plan to let go and forgive.*

2. *Do you still regret missing out on an ample opportunity in your past? If yes, what would happen if you focused on the positive opportunities that have been favorable? Create a list of all the positive outcomes in your life.*

3. *Have you avoided a family, social, or business gathering due to a bitter conflict with another person? If yes, has avoidance worked to improve emotional feelings? Create a plan to attend a future gathering focusing on positive discussions and interactions.*

4. *Do you become emotional when hearing or seeing a story you can relate to? What about the story triggered your emotions?*

Mark 11:25

[25] And when you stand praying, if you hold anything against anyone, forgive them so that your Father in heaven may forgive you your sins.

Affirmations

God's word flows through me.

I forgive myself and others.

I accept that I can only control my actions.

I have let go of my past hurts.

I accept my emotions and allow them to have a purpose.

ANXIETY

Everyone has some form of anxiety. People with social anxiety may appear nervous about heart-to-heart conversations as well. It could be a topic that someone would instead stray away from to avoid feeling sadness. It may remind them of a time in their life that wasn't pleasant.

I have a fear of driving over bridges. It's a fear that I developed later in my life. This is something I've been working on overcoming. When approaching a bridge thoughts and feelings become overwhelming. I have worked on changing my thoughts from feeling like I would fall off the bridge to it's just a little road over water. I believed in myself and am slowly gaining control of my thoughts. In the past I've been in the car driving with my husband and family before and decided to pull over so someone else could drive. Still today I am working on ways to overcome this anxiety. I found a few remedies to help. I take longer routes to avoid bridges. I also found myself using strategies such as listening to music really loud when crossing bridges as a distraction. I'll even start off-the-cuff conversations with my husband to shift my thoughts. My husband has been a gift to me as he's been that friend to talk me over many bridges. Each day I'm learning new methods to overcome anxiety. I have become better at refocusing my thoughts in a way to control my adrenaline.

In addition to driving over bridges, I've been anxious when speaking in public. I thought, how am I going to do this? Why am I asked to speak? Will they understand me? These were all questions I've asked myself. Sweat used to appear everywhere before I spoke in front of audiences. It would be visible all over my palms and upper lip. The only thing I did not do was faint. I often rambled out of nervousness. Over time, I learned to control my anxiety and bodily responses. When preparing to speak in front of an audience, a brown paper bag becomes my pre-game calming agent. It's kind of funny when you visualize it but it works for me. I simply pull out the small paper bag and I will then breathe in and out into the bag. This helps control my breathing to avoid hyperventilating while calming my anxiety. It's okay to giggle, call me the brown paper bag lady but it works. Find what works for you to control anxiety. I recommend finding something that'll bring you peace and that will make you smile.

Questions for the Readers

1. What bring on your anxiety?

2. Are you afraid to take on new projects or ventures? Why?

3. What methods have you used to overcome anxiety?

4. Do you feel that your anxiety will get in the way of your success? Why?

Psalm 91:4-6

[4]*He will cover you with his feathers, and under his wings, you will find refuge; his faithfulness will be your shield and rampart.* [5]*You will not fear the terror of night,* [6]*nor the arrow that flies by day, nor the pestilence that stalks in the darkness, nor the plague that destroys at midday.*

Affirmations

I have created a safe and secure space for myself.

I am courageous and will move through doors of opportunity.

I am optimistic that God will work in my favor.

I have everything I need to succeed.

WHAT THEY SAY DOESN'T MATTER

It doesn't matter what they say about you! You were created in God's image. Think about that for a moment. You have allowed other people's words upset you when you are perfect in God's eyes.

Don't dwell on what others may think. How many times have you delayed your progress due to insecurity? Don't allow your insecurities to kill your dreams for success. Make your insecurities work for you. Be secure in who you are. Be firm in what you stand for. What is your passion? Make up your mind that you want it. All you need to do is have confidence in yourself. That is all that matters.

I believed that beauty passed me by. I thought because I grew up in an environment where light-skinned African-American women with long hair were celebrated and brown-skinned darker women with short hair were not celebrated. The fear of not being accepted because of my looks was hard. I came from a family of beautiful brown-skinned women. However, I could not embrace brown-skinned women as being beautiful because they were not celebrated. The media, celebrities, my fellow schoolmates, peers, and even some family members praised the looks of thin, lighter-skinned women. I can recall being called names by other black people regarding my complexion and weight. The Dark One, Black tar-baby, Spook, and Blackie were a few of the names that I and others were called. Imagine hearing these words and hearing them from even your own family.

Then one day I met Ms. Dark and Lovely. She was my cousin's girlfriend. She was a dark brown-skinned woman, with a stylish shorter-cut hair. She was gorgeous, and she celebrated her darkness. I am unsure of the reason, but I felt liberated when I met her. I honestly believe it had much to do with the respect, attention, and love I saw my cousin show her. She also did not show any care for what anyone thought of her, her complexion, style nor attitude. Whenever I see Ms. Dark and Lovely, I smile because she helped me. She was a model to me and showed me how to be confident in my dark brown skin.

One day I thought about all the hurtful names I had been called over the years. Then I thought about the people that called me those names. I laughed to myself because as I thought about it, I let the words of broken people control me. The people that called me and others those names where ignorant to the effects of their words. They were broken people that used me and others as an outlet for their pain. I didn't love myself nor had confidence in myself because I believed every negative word said about me. Today however I smile each morning when I look in the mirror. I am one full-figured, brilliant, chocolate woman, and I embrace who I am. I love myself and who I have become; what they said never mattered is what my mother has always said. She was right. Beauty never passed me by because it was always in me.

Close your eyes and mentally stamp an image of your best self. Focus on that visual now and whenever you need a boost of confidence. That image is of a person who only sees the best in you. Another person's negative words about you, your goals, and your life do not matter. You are inspired by the positivity that motivates you to become a successful person. Hopefully, you've realized that people who hurt people make you their verbal punching bag to release their pain. Ignore these people if they bring you pain, and surround yourself with positive people who celebrate you.

Questions for the Readers

1. Are you distracted by the opinions of others? Why are the opinions of others important?

2. What are your best qualities?

3. When was the last time you complimented yourself?

4. When was the last time you complimented a stranger?

1 Peter 3:3-4

³Your beauty should not come from outward adornment, such as elaborate hairstyles and the wearing of gold jewelry or fine clothes. ⁴Rather, it should be that of your inner self, the unfading beauty of a gentle and quiet spirit, which is of great worth in God's sight.

Affirmations

I am focused on what is essential in my journey.

I have permission to do what is right for me.

I am beautiful inside and out.

I am living a positive life.

Positive words about myself and others flow from my heart.

FREDDI T. LANE

BE BOLD

Be bold. You cannot gain success without boldly taking action. You have to be brave. Be confident enough in yourself to operate in your boldness, whether it's speaking your truth boldly or boldly launching a business. What does it mean to you to be bold? Does bold mean courageous and daring?

When were you told to be bold, and what did it mean? How does boldness make you feel? Be bold when you're promoting yourself. Remember, no one can promote you how you can promote yourself. It's about standing out. Recognize that you are unique.

In 2018, we launched my daughter's beauty and skin care product line. The skin care products were made of all-natural ingredients. I feared I was putting too much pressure on my 16-year-old to sprint into the business world. She was a junior in high school. However, I saw greatness in her to dominate beauty and skin care products in our region. My daughter told me about her fears of failing two days before our store's grand opening. She said she did not want to participate in her store's grand opening. She was afraid that her products would not sell.

On the other hand, I was more than confident that the products would sell based on the success of pre-order sales. My daughter looked defeated and physically ill on our two-hour drive to Richmond, Virginia, for the grand opening event. I did not disturb her as I knew she was scared of failing. As we approached the elegant opening venue, I looked at my daughter, and she still had a look of fear. I hugged her and told her that she would do great. As we set up last-minute promotional material, customers surrounded our table. Patrons realized that my daughter was the face of the company and also selling products during the grand opening. I saw a smile on my daughter's face as I looked up. She was boldly talking about the products, telling customers of the benefits of her products. The event was a success and we sold out of products.

Fear is natural; however, it will be hard to sell your dreams and visions if you do not stand in your boldness. Remember to have a bold, ambitious spirit when fulfilling your dream in your business or personal life. The ambition which was embodied when you decided to make your dream a reality needs to be the same ambition that you carry when working through the doubts.

Questions for the Readers

1. *Do your goals energize you? What goal are you most ambitious to complete?*

2. *Are you afraid to publicly display your skill and talents? Create a list of how your skills and talents will help others.*

3. *Do you feel that others do not appreciate you? What are five things that you appreciate about yourself?*

4. *Do you feel you don't have enough knowledge to share what you know? Create a list of free educational resources in your subject matter and create a plan to expand your knowledge.*

1 Corinthians 15:58
[58]Therefore, my dear brothers and sisters, stand firm. Let nothing move you. Always give yourselves entirely to the work of the Lord because you know that your labor in the Lord is not in vain.

FREDDI T. LANE

Affirmations

I am full of brilliant ideas.

I will show and share my talents with others.

I am full of God's love, joy, and abundance.

I am a powerhouse of wealth and knowledge.

44

FREDDI T. LANE

EAT SOME HUMBLE PIE

The COVID-19 Pandemic hit the world hard in 2020. My first outing, once travel bans were lifted, was a trip to a women's retreat in Clearwater, Florida. I attended as a participant. Following almost two years of isolation, I wanted to meet new people and take advantage of the mind, body, and spiritual clinics they offered at the retreat. I conversed with other participants during one of the morning workout sessions. One of the women asked me how I found out about the retreat and what made me sign up. I responded that I sought out the group to meet new people. I also explained that I'd recently moved from the northeast to the area and did not know anyone. During our conversation, she told me her daughter attended college in my hometown. That connection led to further discussions. It was fulfilling; I gained a feeling of strength from this woman. I liked her. The day carried on, and everyone completed the morning workout session. Then, we all headed back to our hotel to freshen up. We enjoyed a day of reflecting on the retreat. We had personal time for ourselves before the evening ceremony and dinner.

After preparing for the formal ceremony, I entered the ballroom of our hotel. The ballroom had been transformed for the occasion. There were decorations and a waiting staff lined up and ready to serve. I looked around the room. All I could see was a room filled with 50 gorgeous women. Seeing women from all backgrounds come together to celebrate wellness made me smile. After eating dinner, the mistress of ceremonies introduced the special guest speaker. I was in awe. Who knew that the woman I conversed with earlier would be the speaker for the evening? There she was, the Honorable Judge Mary S. Scriven. She began talking, and I teared up a little. So many emotions hit me at once. Her story and struggles moved me. She was relatable and took the time to interact with little old me. Judge Mary S. Scriven was the first African American woman as the U.S. District Court Judge for the Middle District of Florida.

Over the years, I've interacted with people across broad platforms. The interaction that I shared with Judge Scriven was the most memorable one. She was humble. As a guest of honor, I thought she would've sat in the front of the room throughout the conference. I am so used to seeing people of a certain status as untouchable. No, this was not the case for Judge Scriven. She sat out in the audience as a participant during the entire workshop. She participated in the retreat the same way as the rest of us. I'm not saying that her status or career was insignificant, but she did not separate herself from the rest of us. She did not overtalk or fight to be seen. She did not know it all. She showed vulnerability in her participation. She was down-to-earth and relatable, and she looked like me. Many others could learn from her kindness, humility, and humbleness.

Questions for the Reader

1. *Do you find it hard to release controls and accept help from others? Create a list of daily, weekly, or monthly chores. Solicit the use of a family member or close friend to help you with that chore. How did it make you feel?*

2. *What was your most humbling experience? What did you learn from that experience?*

3. *Are you able to be a champion for yourself and others?* If so, how? Give ten examples

1 Peter 3:8-9

[8]Finally, all of you, be like-minded, sympathetic, love one another, be compassionate and humble. [9]Do not repay evil with evil or insult with insult. On the contrary, repay evil with blessing because to this you were called so that you may inherit a blessing.

Affirmations

I will allow myself space to grow and learn from others.

I surrender, so I'm able to love others.

I appreciate the intimacy shared between myself and others.

I am healthy.

I'm thankful for another day.

ACKNOWLEDGMENTS

First and foremost, I thank God. He is the reason for my existence. God continually gives me strength, vision, and ambition. Honestly, if it weren't for my husband, this book wouldn't exist. He's supported my desire to speak to the masses, even if it is between a front and back book cover. Thank you for allowing me in your book world. I've learned in many ways from your journey and now my own. This book world tends to influence relationships; however, it is up to us to determine in what direction we want those relationships to go. At the beginning and end of the day, it's all about embodying respectful relationships.

My parents' voices have been my internal editors. Their work ethic and wisdom have steered me in many directions. As parents often do, they wanted me to do as they desired. However, they allowed me to be a rebel and make my own decisions. In some cases, I returned to them to help clean up my mess which they did but never without the "I told you so" speech. Thank you for allowing me to "figure it out" to make it work!

Fam Bam, thank you for allowing me to learn from you. You all are intelligent, clear thinkers with great spirits. I hope we've planted seeds of independence to get you to the next step without the fear of asking for help. I get to watch you all take on the world. Continue to grow in greatness. I love each of you for helping me grow.

Freddi T. Lane

ABOUT THE AUTHOR

Freddi T. Lane is a mother, wife, daughter, friend, life coach, and motivational speaker. Having over 25 years of experience in public service she is passionate about helping minorities get to the next level. Freddi T. Lane is one of the biggest supporters of entrepreneurship and developing strong businesses. Her primary goal is to help others believe in themselves and their God-given abilities. This is the first of many books to come from Freddi T. Lane.

.

NOTES

_____

_____

_____

_____

_____

_____

_____

_____

_____

_____

_____

_____

_____

_____

_____

_____

_____

_____

_____

FREDDI T. LANE

FREDDI T. LANE

FREDDI T. LANE

_____

_____

_____

_____

_____

_____

_____

_____

_____

_____

_____

_____

_____

_____

_____

_____

_____

_____

_____

FREDDI T. LANE

FREDDI T. LANE

FREDDI T. LANE

_____

_____

_____

_____

_____

_____

_____

_____

www.ingramcontent.com/pod-product-compliance
Lightning Source LLC
Chambersburg PA
CBHW071904020426
42331CB00010B/2668